THOMAS BEWICK

THOMAS BEWICK

Selected Work

*Edited with an introduction and notes
by Robyn Marsack*

FyfieldBooks

First published in Great Britain 1989 by
Carcanet Press Ltd
208-212 Corn Exchange Limited
Manchester M4 3BQ

British Library Cataloguing in Publication Data

Bewick, Thomas, *1753-1828*
    Selected Works.
    1. English wood engravings. Bewick,
    Thomas, 1753-1828, illustrations
    I. Title II. Marsack, Robyn
    769.92'4

    ISBN 0 85635 780 4

The publisher acknowledges financial assistance
from the Arts Council of Great Britain

Typeset in 10pt Palatino by Bryan Williamson, Manchester
Printed and bound in England by BAS Printers, Ltd, Hampshire

Contents

Introduction

'A work of art is a corner of nature seen through a temperament.'
– Emile Zola

Thomas Bewick was, it seems, a sociable, down-to-earth, argumentative, stubborn, affectionate family man, 'the best whistler in England', a Whig who also had his touch of Romantic temperament:

> I then took a long walk, backward and forward at the end of the burial ground – listing to the roars of the dashing surge below – this on the one side and the frail memorials of the silent dead on the other – disposed the mind to contemplation and solemn meditation – after this I went home & was sure to meet with what I *call a scold at home* "now Thomas what can you mean by walking among gravestones in the dark night alone I'm sure it is an odd fancy" &c...

That vivid rendition of domestic tone, combined with an intense, solitary reflectiveness is a verbal vignette which parallels the engravings. Bewick's work has always been prized, but its form has somehow excluded it from general histories of art and confined it to monographs and studies of wood-engraving. It answers to many of Pevsner's defining criteria in *The Englishness of English Art*: a preference for observed fact and personal experience, moderation rather than grandeur, and especially a love of what is small and exquisite, shown elsewhere in English watercolours, miniatures, carved misericords. Yet Bewick goes unmentioned by Pevsner, as by John Barrell in his study of the rural poor in English painting, *The Dark Side of the Landscape*, with which his work is a natural point of comparison. Along the line Barrell traces from portrayals of the 'happy husbandman', that cheerful and industrious peasantry of merry England, to those of the 'labouring poor', their rags and poverty a matter of aesthetic interest and pity, Bewick pursues a strongly individual course, while his own scenes of rural life cannot be entirely separated from the intel-

7

lectual currents of the time.

Unlike the great artists of his day – William Blake is his contemporary, John Constable a generation younger – Bewick had no formal artistic training, and his early exposure to art was limited to 'the Kings Arms in the Church, & the signs in Ovingham of the Black Bull, the White Horse, the Salmon & the Hounds & Hare,' and to those prints hanging in every cottage and farmhouse when he was a boy, representations of battles, portraits of distinguished men, 'the sailor's farewell & his happy return – youthfull sports & the feats of Manhood . . . the four seasons &c'. There was no public exhibition of fine arts in Newcastle until 1822. But his childhood provided Bewick with sufficient subjects to last him a lifetime.

He was born at Cherryburn, Eltringham, in Northumberland in August 1753, one of the eight children of Jane (née Wilson, who had been housekeeper to the minister at Ovingham, a village nearby) and John Bewick, a farmer and tenant of a land-sale colliery, that is, where coal is sold direct to local people. There is a colliery (on a larger scale than his father's) in the tailpiece on p.109, across the river from the stately hall. The flat-bottomed boat – a keel – is for carrying coal down the Tyne, beached on the landing stage beside one gesticulating and one contemplative figure. Although smoke billows across from the colliery, it soon blends with the clouds: Bewick seems to accept both sides of the landscape, and indeed was not opposed to the manufacturing and technological advances of the period. He remarks in his *Memoir* that he worked on engraving plans for the proposed Newcastle to Carlisle canal, *c*.1796, but that 'the whole *scheme* of this great, *this important national as well as local undertaking*, was baffled and set aside . . . as in almost every other case, private interest is & was found to over power public good.'

From earliest boyhood, however, his delight lay in the countryside and its pursuits; he was harshly disciplined at school, but that memory is crowded aside by all the wild hours of freedom: 'I was scarcely ever out of an Action either good or bad . . . at one time, in imitation of the Savages described in

"Robinson Crusoe"... I often, in a morning, set off *stark naked* across the Fell, where I was joined by some Associates, who in like manner ran about like mad things...'. Hunting was his first love, for foxes and hares, the badger at night and the foumart (polecat, see p.39) in the snow. The cruelty of the sport 'came upon me at last':

> ... the first time I felt the change, happened by my having (in hunting) caught the Hare in my Arms, while surrounded by the Dogs & the Hunters, when the poor terrified creature screemed out so piteously, like a child, that I would have given anything to save its life; in this however I was prevented, for a Farmer, well known to me, who stood close by, pressed upon me & desired I would give her to him, & from his being better able (as I thought) to save its life, I complied with his wishes; this was no sooner done than he proposed...to have a "bit more sport with her" and this was to be done by his first breaking one of its legs, and then again setting the poor Animal off... [I] learned with pleasure that their intended victim had made its escape.

Compassion struck him later with regard to birds, when he mortally injured a bullfinch: 'this was the last Bird I killed but' – Bewick adds ruefully – 'many indeed have been killed since on my Account', referring to the specimens sent him for the *History of British Birds*. Fishing he loved. And from the time he first had access to paper, or stone floors, he filled all available spaces with his drawings. A friend took pity on his hot chalking on the hearth stone and provided paper:

> pen and Ink and the juice of the Brambleberry made a *grand change* – These were succeeded by a camel hair pencil & Shells of colours and thus supplied I became completely set up – but of Patterns or drawings I had none – the Beasts & Birds which enlivened the beautiful Scenery of Woods & Wilds, surrounding my native Hamlet, furnished me with an endless supply of Subjects.

If he did not read much, he listened a great deal, and principally he heard the old ballads and tales of war. This was, after all, not a stable period of British history. Culloden was fought in 1746, and in Bewick's border region, skirmishes with the Scots were still fresh in men's memories. Bewick says that he listened to the details of battles with the same passionate enthusiasm with which they were related, having not yet 'reasoned myself into a detestation of War'. He must have educated his own children in the latter sentiment: Jane Bewick comments on the tailpiece showing an ass rubbing itself against a battle column, 'A proper use at last of all warlike monuments' (see p.68). The *Memoir* is packed with village characters, including one John Cowie who described the 'minute particulars of the battle of Minden' (in the Seven Years' War) and occasionally wore his old military coat: 'after he died, this coat, which had been shot at both at Minden & else where, was, at last, hung up – on a Stake on the corn Rigs as a scare Crow.' We can see it in the tailpiece on p.63. Bewick was also regaled with stories of 'Phantoms and supernatural things' and knew men 'both old and young, who dared encounter any danger, yet in this way were *affraid of their own Shadows*' – a late tailpiece shows a dog similarly alarmed, and others depict 'Ghosts Boggles Apparitions &c' at men's backs.

His father's matter-of-fact approach to such superstition forced Thomas to overcome his fears: his mother's lectures on religion made little impression, but 'my father's pithy illustrations...were much more forcably and clearly made out. I understood them well & their effect operated powerfully upon me – '. By the time Bewick was fourteen, these would have been parting admonitions, as at that age he was apprenticed to Ralph Beilby, an engraver in Newcastle upon Tyne. The separation from his parents was painful, even more so the initiation into town life, although Newcastle at the time had many pleasant gardens and retained its medieval city wall almost intact. It took Bewick about three hours to walk home to Cherryburn, which he did as often as possible. He was proud of the regime he imposed upon himself, modelled on

Luigi Cornaro's manual of *Sure and Certain Methods of Attaining a Long and Healthful Life.*

Beilby, then twenty-four, had the only general engraving business in a flourishing town – among other things, he dealt with door plates and coffin plates, shop bills and bank notes, crests and designs on silver, crests on books, engraving on glass – and thus had a range of customers and work that was to be immensely beneficial to Bewick. During his seven years' apprenticeship he made the acquaintance of several booksellers and binders, among them Gilbert Gray – a kindly counsellor to many young apprentices – and his son William, who bound books for gentlemen and encouraged Bewick to read them, which he did before his own work began in the morning. There was also George Gray, eminent painter of fruit, botanist, geologist, extensively travelled in North America, whose portrait of Bewick as a young man now hangs in the Laing Gallery, Newcastle upon Tyne. Through the Grays, Bewick met Thomas Spence, who wanted to reform English spelling ('The Kurfu tolz thi Nel ov parting Da') as well as the British Constitution, and for whose new alphabet Bewick cut the steel punches. Exposure to these inventive, questioning minds enlivened a period of exacting and not always rewarding work.

Nevertheless, when Bewick came to the end of his apprenticeship and went home to liberty, he found that even endless angling palled. In 1776 he set off for a 350-mile walk around Scotland: fifty years later he wrote to a friend that he often 'reflected with rapture upon the geniune hospitality I met with during my *wild-goose chase* in the Highlands – when, in the hey day of youth, like an unbridled wild colt I *zig-zaged* them in every direction –'. Meanwhile, Ralph Beilby had sent to the Society for the Encouragement of Arts – set up the year Bewick was born – some wood engravings by Bewick for John Gay's *Fables*, which won him a premium from the Society. In the autumn of 1776, therefore, Bewick determined to try his luck in London, where he already had contacts.

He spent only nine months in London, and it was not until 1828 that he visited the city again. In 1803 he wrote to a friend,

'I would rather be herding sheep on Mickley bank top than remain in London, although for doing so I was to be made Premier of England.' He was not tempted by the variety of 'excellent performances in every art and science', nor by the prospect of unlimited work. He may have had to concentrate much more upon fashionable copperplate engraving had he remained under the aegis of Isaac Taylor, whose masterpiece was his illustrations to Richardson's *Sir Charles Grandison*. Taylor was so put out by his defection that he never spoke or wrote to Bewick again. 'I could not help it... The Country of my old friends – the manners of the people of that day – the scenery of Tyne side, seemed altogether to form a paradise for me & I longed to see it again.'

Bewick could have turned to working by himself, relying on commissions from London as well as Newcastle, and in his *Memoir* he regrets that he did not do so. A mutual friend suggested that he go into partnership with Beilby, which lasted from 1777 to 1797, when it came to an acrimonious end over credit for the texts of *Quadrupeds* and *British Birds*. (Bewick quarrelled not only with his partner, but also with printers and apprentices; his account books show as well that he gave charitably when asked.) Beilby had no facility with woodcuts, and left any work of the sort to Bewick, who experimented successfully with cuts for children's books (see p.27), published by Thomas Saint in Newcastle.

Woodcuts at this period were used mainly to illustrate cheap publications – broadsides and chap-books, histories and ballads – although they also cropped up as headings and chapter initials in books otherwise illustrated by copperplate engravings. The connoisseur Horace Walpole dismissed the woodblocks of his day (*c.* 1770) as 'slovenly stamps'. There were some models available to Bewick, but he gives scant credit to the French and German schools; in an undated draft letter he states: 'I have heard of Papillon and of his abilities in his profession but never saw any of his works, & except Albert Durer I have not seen many of the productions of artists on wood.' This is a rather disingenuous claim: he took French lessons, and the text of Jean-Michel Papillon's *Traité Historique et pratique de la gravure au bois*, in which the skilful engraver advocates the use of end-grained wood, may not have been beyond his grasp; certainly there are some likenesses to Papillon's work in his own. The work of Elisha Kirkall, whose engravings (on metal) illustrated Samuel Croxall's influential *Fables of Aesop and others* (1722), is the admitted model for the engravings produced by Bewick and his brother John for *Select Fables, in Three Parts* (1784). The book goes unmentioned in his *Memoir*, but shows a clear advance on the earlier work, particularly in the handling of landscape.

The increasing technical superiority of Bewick's work to that of his contemporaries is due to his refinement – not invention, as earlier critics maintained – of the process of cutting. Whereas the woodcuts of previous centuries were made on wood planed with the grain, and cut with knives, by the eighteenth century the method of planing across the grain and using metal engraver's tools (rather than the woodcutter's knife) had been discovered. Bewick used boxwood, a very hard wood that grows slowly and reaches only eight or nine inches in diameter. It was sliced, as Iain Bain describes, 'like a cucumber, across the grain, and had to be left to season for some time before it could be used.' He made his own tools for the process of 'white-line' engraving. To quote A. Hyatt Major's brief description: 'In the upstanding fibres he ploughed white lines... Parallel grooves in the end grain make two white lines with a wall between for printing a black line that will not break down, though knife-thin, because the fibres row up as strong as pickets in a fence.' Bewick got his effects by varying the width of these lines and not by cross-hatching (as Dürer had done). He made preliminary pencil studies (and also, independently, exquisite watercolours), which he transferred to the woodblock by blackening the back of the paper with a soft pencil, then tracing the basic outline, leaving a silvery line on the block. All the detail, however, was freehand. Ruskin comments that wood engraving always involves 'ideas of power and dexterity, but also of restraint, and the delight you take in it

13

should involve the understanding of the difficulty the workman dealt with'. Bewick's friend Dovaston described his manner of working as 'absolutely indefatigable; even sometimes sitting at work at a table by the window, while his friends are drinking wine. It is curious to see his economy of boxwood...should there there be a flaw or a decayed spot, he contrives to bring that into a part of the drawing that is to be white, so that it will cut out.'

Bewick's close supervision of the printing process was essential to the delicacy and tonal variety of his engravings. The difficulties of shaping contemporary methods to his needs, the trouble in getting the correct paper, the training of trade pressmen in Newcastle (he would not send the work to London), are frequent causes of frustration and fiery impatience in his letters and the *Memoir*. He was very skilled at 'lowering': by lowering parts of the block before engraving them – for instance, the breast of a bird – he ensured that they would receive less ink and less pressure when printed, and would thus be lighter. The edges of a vignette were slightly lowered so that there was no hard edge when printed. The quality of prints naturally varied, and Bewick invited special customers to select sheets individually before binding them as a book.

In general, sheets for Bewick's books were given out to several local bookbinders, and some were sold to local booksellers who in turn would sell them to gentlemen who had them bound to their own designs. Although he printed a large portion on cheaper paper to make them affordable, the cheapest version of the second edition of *British Birds* (vol.I, 1799) was 10/6, while the most expensive was 21/-; this was at a time when Bewick's trained apprentices were paid 5/- a week on average. The late eighteenth century saw a boom in book production, partly because the London booksellers had lost their battle for perpetual copyright in a legal decision of 1774, and the market was thus open to provincial booksellers (who were also the publishers) to distribute editions of the classics and to reprint proven bestsellers. Alongside them were the flourishing circulating libraries: there was one next to Beilby's original workshop, advertising 'above Two Thousand Volumes on all branches of Polite Literature To be Lent out to Read, at Two Shillings and Sixpence *per* Quarter in the Town and Three Shillings in the Country'. A distinct market for children's books was also emerging.

'Having from the time that I was a school Boy, been displeased with most of the cuts in children's books, & particularly with those of [*A Description of Three Hundred Animals viz., Beasts, Birds, Fishes, Serpents and Insects*] the figures of which, even at that time, I thought I could depicture much better...', Bewick reached a decision to attempt his own publication, in partnership with Beilby and with the encouragement of Solomon Hodgson, bookseller and editor of the *Newcastle Chronicle*. Thus in 1785 he began engraving *A General History of Quadrupeds*. In the *Memoir* he states that the first engraving was done on the day his father died, 15 November, but the original manuscript records his beginning a fortnight later: 'Novr 1785 29 – Begun the Natural History with the Fig of the Dromedary Decr 2d The Camel...'. Bewick's mother died in February of the next year, and in April 1786 he married Isabella Elliot of Ovingham, with whom he had four children and, he says in the *Memoir*, 'a life time of uninterrupted happiness'.

Perhaps it was the cessation of those regular trecks home, and his settling into family life in Newcastle that gave Bewick the space for his new project – although it must be remembered that all such engraving was done after the day's business – and some of the impetus to the vignettes, recording hours of rural observation.

Work on the *Quadrupeds* was interrupted by one major commission: the engraving of the Chillingham Bull for Marmaduke Tunstall of Wycliffe (see pp. 28-9). As paintings from the period show, livestock portraiture was an immensely popular genre, enhancing the owner's status as a breeder: the grander the animal, the better. Indeed Bewick once lost a commission for refusing to 'put lumps of fat here & there to please them where I could not see it.' Copies of the bull engraving were rare, as the woodblock was damaged after only a few impressions. Tunstall paid £7.7.0 for what Bewick considered to be one of his best works. Douglas Bliss, in his *History of Wood Engraving*, calls it a 'technical triumph'. When he qualifies this by saying that the wood engraving is 'too rich in texture, deficient in colour [i.e. tonal range], obvious in pattern', it should be remembered that Bewick was keen to show that he could compete with the copper engravers on their own terms, particularly in matters such as the dense texture of foliage.

By the mid-eighteenth century, natural history was all the rage; Bewick's decision was scarcely a gamble. The *Critical Review* of 1763 had declared that 'Natural History is now, by a kind of *national establishment*...the favourite study of the time'; the reading public was avid for something readable, factual and elegant, to which the subject, illustrated, lent itself. The most popular volumes of all were the Comte de Buffon's *Histoire naturelle* (1749-1804; first translated into English in 1762), later edited by Dr Smellie in nine volumes (1781-5; the edition known to Bewick); Oliver Goldsmith's *History of the Earth and Animated Nature* (1774); Gilbert White's *Natural History of Selborne* (1789). In his Preface to *British Birds*, Bewick remarks of Buffon 'that in many instances that ingenious philosopher has overstepped the bounds of Nature...too frequently hurried into the wild paths of conjecture and romance'; White, however, greatly pleased him. Exploration abroad and investigations at home were increasing the contemporary stock of knowledge; there were dozens of natural history exhibitions. This meant that although Bewick had to rely on pictures in Smellie's edition for his most exotic species, he was able to see living examples of a variety of monkeys, a tiger, a lion and a porcupine brought to Newcastle in 1788. He also asked his brother John, now in London, to provide drawings of the animals to which he had access.

In organizing the book, he followed Buffon's model of 'kinds', groups of structurally similar animals, and devoted a high proportion to domestic breeds – thirty-nine pages to sheep, seventeen to dogs, for example – because, as the Advertisement states, they 'so materially contribute to the strength, the wealth, and the happiness of this Kingdom'. Harriet Ritvo suggests that the unstated argument of the book is embodied in this system of classification: nature, no longer to be feared, could be ordered in a rational, comprehensible way that emphasized the creation of animals for man's benefit, in a hierarchy that stressed human authority, divinely ordained.

Such self-confidence is tempered, however, by the tailpieces, which show man as less noble and less masterly than Ritvo's argument implies, and more at the mercy of the elements. See the tailpiece on p.40 for example, where a man defecates behind a bush, and the woman holds her nose against the combined odours of man, pipe, and kiln in the background. Or instances of man's inhumanity: the boy leading two blind fiddlers (p.50), his hat out for alms, oblivious to the warning on the rich man's wall – 'Steel Traps – Spring Guns'. The first edition of *Quadrupeds* was published in 1790; Bewick made additions to the seven subsequent editions, and perhaps it is not altogether fanciful to see in his depiction of domestic cruelties a parallel with continental upheavals.

For Bewick, Newcastle was by no means a backwater. Certainly he lived a very regular life there, with only a few excursions, until his death in 1828. He rose at six, sometimes earlier, and took a walk; he was rarely outside the house after 10 p.m., when he had his bread and cheese, with a glass of ale or rum and hot water. Each day on the way to his workshop he would stop off to hear the news of the morning: in 1794, he was sufficiently distressed by the political situation in his 'own much-loved land' to 'bend his mind towards America...'. Before his marriage he was a member of Swarley's Club – the ticket of admission, engraved by Beilby, calls it 'The Newcastle House of Lords' – and later of the Brotherly Society. For Swarley's he paid 4d, to be spent on beer only, and the conversations there between merchants and tradesmen only broke up 'at the time when the War on behalf [of] despotism was raging & the Spy system was set afloat'. At the Blue Bell he mixed with 'men of sense and consequence', 'a set of staunch advocates for the liberty of mankind', who 'set the example of

17

propriety of conduct to those of a more violent turn of mind, but indeed the political enormities of the times excited the indignation of many & which it was not easy to keep within due bounds.'

Such indignation surfaces in the *Memoir*, written at the end of Bewick's life but not published until thirty-four years after his death, when it caused admirers of his work to deplore the chapters on religious and political matters. (Charles Kingsley and John Ruskin were warm in their praise of the book.) To the modern reader, however, they make a great deal of sense: the misuse of their privileges by rich landowners, the hypocrisy and sectarianism of organized religion, the 'superlative wickedness' of Pitt's war against France, sensible notions of children's education, hatred of the Enclosure Acts – all this we find sympathetic. Writing to Dovaston in 1826, Bewick recalls the bunches of broom or heather which used to indicate places on the fells where ale was sold:

> ... the only Sign then used on the Fells, by path sides, on undivided Grounds – but they are now *divided by Act of Parliament*, and added to the lands of such as had too much before – & the broad shouldered Sunburnt healthy unpolluted and brave Inhabitants, of their wastes & their Cots & garths, are now all swept away – these were the 'bold peasantry, a Countries pride' where are they now?

The voice is his own – undoubtedly a sample of those reflections of which 'he generally relieved his powerful mind in the bosom of his very aimiable family', as Dovaston recorded – but is also that of the non-gentry, non-metropolitan mind we find in the poetry of the period; concerned with social documentation, and with strong local loyalties. William Cowper and George Crabbe in the 1780s; Burns too, of course, with whom Ruskin compared Bewick; Wordsworth in the 1790s; John Clare in the 1820s. Wordsworth paid enthusiastic tribute to Bewick's art in 'The Two Thieves': in the manuscript version 'the Poet who lives on the banks of the Tyne' is compared to Reynolds, to the latter's disadvantage; in the published version of 1800 the comparison is omitted, and the poem opens, 'O now that the genius of Bewick were mine...'. Bewick's *Land Birds* was published in 1797, the year before the *Lyrical Ballads*.

The success of the *Quadrupeds* encouraged Bewick to this new project, *A History of British Birds*, which he began in 1791. It also brought him commissions from printers and publishers throughout the country, notably from the Newcastle man William Bulmer, who had established his Shakspeare Press in London. Thomas, and John Bewick – whose skill was considerable – engraved for Bulmer *The Poems of Goldsmith and Parnell*, the handsomest of contemporary volumes of Bewick's work. The engravings were not as good as those for *British Birds*, nevertheless their delicacy was such that some doubted they were really wood engravings: 'his late Majesty entertained so great a doubt on the subject that he ordered his bookseller ... to procure the blocks for his inspection...'. The brothers also illustrated Somervile's *Chase*, published in 1796, after John Bewick's death at the age of thirty-five. Bewick felt that he had been exploited by Bulmer, and did no further work for him.

Bewick's years of observing birds – feeding them was an unusual practice for the period – made these volumes an even more personal work than the *Quadrupeds*. Bird-watchers up and down the country supplied him with information, indeed with birds. At first he drew from stuffed examples collected by Marmaduke Tunstall for his Wycliffe museum, but British methods of stuffing birds lagged behind those on the Continent, and not all of the specimens would have looked natural or retained the colours of their plumage. His cash-books record the traffic in fresher specimens: 'Sea-gull from Tynemouth -/-/2 ... Carriage of an Owl from Wallington -/-/2 ... Carriage of a box from Cambridge pr mail inclosing 2 white sparrows 3/10/- ... 3 Birds stinking sent per W. Losh...'. The developing British passion for ornithology meant the abandonment in many quarters of guns in favour of telescopes or spy-glasses; Bewick's own telescope marked 1794 is preserved at the Wildfowl Trust, Slimbridge, and he remarks on the information

Dovaston gathered by this means. As Iain Bain points out, Bewick's greatest successes are with familiar subjects such as the garden birds, and his greatest difficulties with swimming birds, where he did not resolve the 'problem of trying to combine the information relating to the bird's feet and their use in the bird's natural environment'. To each new edition (by 1826 there were eight editions of *Land Birds* and six editions of *Water Birds*, first published in 1804), Bewick added birds or tailpieces, replaced old cuts, and repaired damage done in the press. Thomas Hugo, in his otherwise inaccurate *Bewick Collector* (1866, 1868), observed that the blackbird's beak had been replaced six times.

He could not keep up with the flood of correspondence. In *The Naturalist in Britain*, D.E. Allen argues that Bewick insufficiently appreciated the volumes' role as text books: 'When a group of Shropshire naturalists sent him the extensive harvest of many years of unusually careful observation for inclusion in the forthcoming sixth edition, he thanked them and proceeded to ignore it almost entirely...'. It should be noted in Bewick's defence that he was probably very tired of the whole revision procedure by this stage. Charles Kingsley wrote to Bewick's daughters after their father's death about his own father's buying the first volume when it came out: '...he was laughed at in the New Forest for having bought a book about "dickie birdies", till his fellow squires borrowing his copy, agreed that it was the most clever book they had ever seen, and a revelation to them...'. The encomium on Bewick in *Blackwood's Edinburgh Magazine* (1825) suggested that a study of Bewick would allow the reader to 'know a British bird as you know a man, by his physiognomy': 'the sleepy-headed gourmand duck; the restless titmouse...the keen rapacious kite...Sir Thomas Lawrence could do no more for the Royal Yacht Club or the Congress of Vienna.'

But it is the tailpieces that have most engaged Bewick's readers. He himself looked on them as instructive to his younger audience: 'I interspersed the more serious studies with *Tale*-pieces of gaiety and humour; yet even in these seldom without

an endeavour to illustrate some truth or point some moral.'
Bewick's spelling underlines their anecdotal quality. Some of
the morals have been preserved in notes by Jane Bewick, such
as the case of the man driving his cow through the river to
save paying the bridge toll (see p.112): he loses his hat, worth
more than the toll. The narrative power of these very detailed,
tiny engravings often derives from suspense: on page 30, for
example, the child is about to pull a horse's tail, the mother
is already running to rescue her from the consequences. Rus-
kin held that it was 'one of the most terrific facts in all the
history of British art that Bewick never draws children but in
mischief.' It is exactly this sense of energy, albeit misdirected
at times, that is magnetic. Even in the stillness of his snow
scenes, something wakes, and his peaceable anglers are poised
for movement. Only the gravestones are incontestably undis-
turbed – though not always undisturbing.

It was the 'Gothic' element of Bewick's imagination that
caught Charlotte Brontë's, in the famous passage at the begin-
ning of *Jane Eyre* when Jane retires behind a curtain with *British
Birds*: 'I cannot tell what sentiment haunted the quite solitary
churchyard with its inscribed headstone; . . . The fiend pinning
down the thief's pack behind him, I passed over quickly: it
was an object of terror' (see p.76). The vignettes also seem to
have been a source for Jane's own enigmatic paintings. This
link with Romantic taste provides a perspective from Bewick
back to medieval illumination, and forward to the Pre-Raphael-
ites. (D.C. Thomson, in his biography, suggests that for the
background to the Chillingham Bull, Bewick 'might in our day
have been styled a Pre-Raphaelite'.) For the Romantics – as
for William Morris – medieval book-making represented an
ideal marriage of text and illustration. Copperplate engravings
had to be printed on special paper and bound in separately,
whereas woodblocks were the same height as type so that text
and picture could be printed together, allowing an integral
relation between the two. In the work of medieval scribes,
scenes of rural life, and especially individual birds and beasts,
could be enclosed by the lettering itself. The vignette works in

the opposite direction: it lacks a border, so opens out into the text, encouraging the play of speculation and imagination. Charles Rosen and Henri Zerner have written a very suggestive essay on this theme, but I am unwilling to push the Romantic notion too far, given Bewick's own preference – recorded by his daughter – for the boxed-in vignette he uses in the *Select Fables of Aesop.*

This was the last completed work of his own publishing – a *History of British Fishes* was not far advanced at his death – and gave him more trouble than the preceding volumes. As with the illustrations made for the *Select Fables* of 1784, these are based on Croxall's designs and ultimately on Francis Barlow's etchings of 1660, but Bewick's drawings of animals are much finer, and there are some excellent tailpieces. His apprentices were involved with this book to a greater extent, perhaps, than with others. Bewick had about eighteen apprentices over his time as master, not all of whom were wood-engravers: Robert Johnson, for example, was a draughtsman and remarkable colourist. Luke Clennell contributed many tailpieces to the second volume of *British Birds*, and Bewick's son Robert drew some fine fishes. (See Bain and Reynolds Stone for discussions of the apprentices' work.) Ruskin, in his lectures on the art of wood engraving, analyses in detail Bewick's illustration of a pig ('he could draw a pig but not a Venus'), and of the frogs in a *Fables'* tailpiece, which he uses as examples of 'the magnificent artistic power, the flawless virtue, veracity, tenderness, – the infinite humour of the man.'

For Ruskin, Bewick was a perfect example of the unschooled native genius; the equal in his drawing to Holbein and Turner, but not a gentleman, with his 'love of ugliness which is in the English soul'. One commentator in 1825 wrote an 'Essay on the Genius of Bewick' which delighted the artist, but made him anxious with its strictures on a couple of 'coarse if not vulgar vignettes' (see pp.110, 118); Jane asked her father to withdraw them. Writing to Dovaston, Bewick declares that virtuous women are 'like the connecting *link between Men and Angels'*, whom he would not dream of offending, 'altho, I think myself that these notions of the ladies, border on the fastidious'. The attempt to tidy up the man's work – like the attempt to tidy up the man himself by editing his *Memoir* – goes deeply against the grain of his vision. Even Ruskin admits that, for all his failings in 'grace and scholarship', Bewick never fails in 'truth and vitality', and he attributes this to Bewick's rootedness in country life. Everything in nature had its intrinsic fascination, it was 'a world in which the dog, the plover, the farmer's wife, the tramp, the old pollard are all personalities to be watched and interpreted without bias in favour of the human species' (Edmund Blunden).

John Barrell notes that there was a remarkable increase in paintings of rural subjects in the 1790s, and that the average number of such paintings exhibited at the Royal Academy remained high throughout the French wars, until 1818. They were seen in a strongly nationalistic light. Let us juxtapose this with the increasing popularity of natural history in general and bird-watching (something that even town-dwellers can do) in particular: perhaps that owed something to a sense that access to the countryside was becoming a little less easy, as towns expanded and the pressures of the industrial revolution began to make themselves felt. Already that dream of pastoral life which has been so potent an image of paradise for artists begins to assume the shape in which, in cruder or glossier versions, it is purveyed today. Martin Wiener, in *English Culture and the Decline of the Industrial Spirit 1850-1980*, has documented the extent to which the revival of village values owes its framework to early twentieth century historians from a wealthy elite, who were rejecting industrial capitalism and redefining what it means to be English.

The danger for Bewick, now, is that his representation of north-country life in Georgian England should be assimilated into a late twentieth century nostalgia that sentimentalizes his tenderness and humour, and dissipates his passionate energy.

Further Reading

Turn first to Bewick's own *Memoir* (Oxford University Press, 1975, 1979), edited and introduced by Iain Bain, which prints the original text for the first time and is unabridged. Bain has also produced a lavishly illustrated and informative record for the Laing Gallery, Newcastle upon Tyne, *Thomas Bewick* (1979). His beautiful edition of *The Watercolours and Drawings of Thomas Bewick and his workshop apprentices* was published in two volumes by Gordon Fraser (London) in 1981. All of these provide much more technical information than there is space for here.

There is one collection of Bewick's engravings in print, the compendious *1800 Woodcuts by Thomas Bewick and his school* (published by Dover Books, New York, 1962; distributed in the UK by Constable). A large percentage of the work in this book is not by Bewick or his apprentices. The reproductions are better in Reynolds Stone's selection, *Wood Engravings of Thomas Bewick*, with a useful introduction by Stone, himself a fine engraver. This was published by Rupert Hart-Davis (London) in 1953 but is unfortunately out of print, as is Montague Weekley's biography of Bewick, published the same year by OUP.

For nineteenth-century works on Bewick, consult the bibliography in Bain's edition of the *Memoir*. Ruskin's remarks may be found in *Aratra Pentelici* (1872), *The Art of England* (1883) and *Ariadne Florentina* (1890). *Bewick to Dovaston: Letters 1824-1828*, edited by Gordon Williams with an introduction by Montague Weekley, is a very lively compilation (Nattali & Maurice Ltd, London, 1968).

For recent essays on Bewick, see: Harriet Ritvo, *The Animal Estate: the English and other creatures in Victorian England* (Harvard University Press, 1987); Charles Rosen and Henri Zerner, *Romanticism and Realism: the mythology of nineteenth century art* (Faber and Faber, London, 1984); Max F. Schulz, *Paradise Preserved: recreations of Eden in eighteenth and nineteenth century England* (Cambridge University Press, 1985). I am indebted to Dr M.A.V. Gill's paper on 'The Beilby and Bewick Workshop', given to the Newcastle Imprint Club on 27 November 1975, a copy of which is deposited in the National Library of Scotland.

More general background may be found in John Barrell, *The Dark Side of the Landscape: the rural poor in English painting 1730-1840* (CUP, 1980); Douglas Percy Bliss, *A History of Wood-Engraving* (J.M. Dent, London, 1928); A Hyatt Major, *Prints and People: a social history of printed pictures* (Princeton University Press, 1971). For the naturalist aspects of Bewick's work see David Elliston Allen, *The Naturalist in Britain: a social history* (Allen Lane, London, 1976); Keith Thomas, *Man and the Natural World: changing attitudes in England 1500-1800* (Penguin, 1984).

Readers may be interested to know that the Cherryburn estate was purchased in 1982 by the charitable Thomas Bewick Birthplace Trust, to house and display valuable original material – including 150 original Bewick woodblocks – and eventually to provide facilities for studying wood engraving from Bewick's time to the present day. The Thomas Bewick Birthplace Museum is at Mickley, Stocksfield, Northumberland NE43 7DB.

A Note on the Engravings

Except for the receipt on p.127 and the copperplate engraving on p.129, which have been reduced by about fifteen per cent, all the engravings are reproduced at their actual size.

For the *Quadrupeds* I have followed the order of vignettes and tailpieces in the edition of 1807 (the fifth). For *British Birds* I have followed approximately the order for the volumes of 1826, i.e. the eighth edition of *Land Birds* and the sixth of *Water Birds*. In many cases the vignette of the bird is followed by the tailpiece assigned to it in those editions, e.g. the yellow owl, the rook, the heron, the redbreast.

As mentioned in the Introduction, Bewick was assisted by apprentices. I have mostly confined the engravings in this selection to those known to be by Bewick, or at least designed by him, but some by apprentices have been included for their intrinsic interest and for comparison. These are indicated in the Notes at the end of the book. Although apprentices engraved the illustrations for *The Fables of Aesop*, Bewick drew very detailed designs on the wood for them to follow, and says that the minutiae required 'close superintendance & help and when the Cuts are done I then go over the whole'.

Acknowledgement

I am particularly grateful to Iain Bain for his generous assistance with this book; my thanks also to Stuart Airlie and Michael Schmidt.

One of Bewick's earliest commissions

from *Fables by the late Mr Gay . . .*

Bewick. *NEWCASTLE 1789*

The Wild B

ingham

The Old English Road-Horse

Tees-Water Old or Unimproved Breed

33

The Rein-Deer

The Stag or Red-Deer

The Fallow-Deer

The Rhinoceros

The Lion

The Tiger

The Stoat

The Foumart

40

The Greyhound Fox

The Cur Fox

The Bull-Dog

The Mastiff

The Dalmatian or Coach Dog

The Irish Greyhound

44

The Old English Hound

The Newfoundland Dog

The Domestic Rabbit

The Squirrel

The Water Rat

The Long-Tailed Field Mouse

The Mole

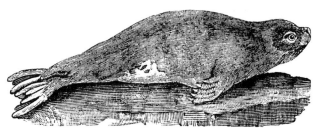

The Seal

54

Esto perpetua!

The Female Kestrel

The Stone Falcon

The Merlin

59

The Long-Eared Owl

The Short-Eared Owl

The Yellow Owl

The Rook

The Magpie

The Jay

The Golden Oriole

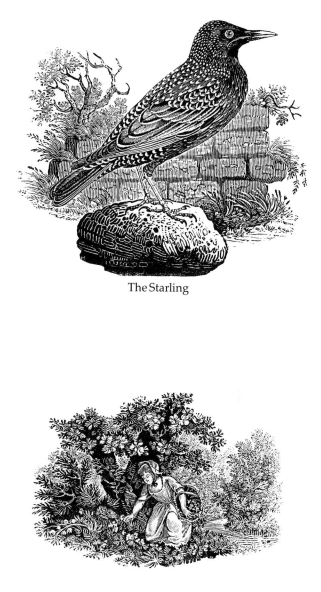

The Starling

The Fieldfare

The Redwing

The Cuckoo

The Pied Woodpecker

The Nuthatch

The Hoopoe

The Green Grosbeak

The Yellow Bunting

The Tawny Bunting

75

The Goldfinch

The Linnet

The Lark

The Woodlark

The Wheatear

The Grey Wagtail

The Dartford Warbler

The Redbreast

The Hedge Warbler

The Reed Warbler

The White-Throat

The Willow-Wren

The Wren

The Whinchat

The Blue Titmouse

The Marsh Titmouse

The Night-Jar

The Ring Dove

The Domestic Cock

The Peacock

The Pintado (Guinea Fowl)

The Red-Legged Partridge

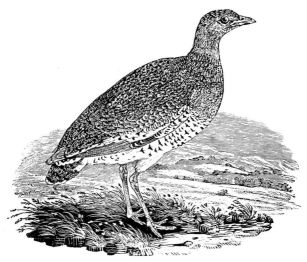

The Little Bustard

The Great Plover

The Ring Dotterel

97

The Heron

The Night Heron

The Bittern

The Snipe

The Godwit

The Greenshank

The Red Sandpiper

The Dunlin

The Turnstone

The Kingfisher

The Spotted Rail or Spotted Gallinule

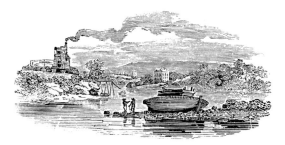

The Black-Backed Gull

113

The Dun-Diver

114

The Smew

The Swan Goose

116

The Mute Swan

The Grey Lag Goose

The Muscovy Duck

The Tame Duck

The Wood Sandpiper

Waiting for Death

Newcastle, January 1, 1824.

To Thomas Bewick & Son D.ʳ

To a Royal Copy of Esop's Fables £ 1 . 4 . —

Received the above with thanks

Thomas Bewick,   *Robert Elliot Bewick*

Thomas Bewick

his   *mark*

127

T. Bewick & Son.

Mr Culley's Beagles

——will Hunt at ——

PLACE	DAY	HOUR
_____	Monday	_____ o'Clock
_____	Tuesday	_____ D.º
_____	Wednesday	_____ D.º
_____	Thursday	_____ D.º
_____	Friday	_____ D.º
_____	Saturday	_____ D.º

WHITHAM

A Cheviot Ram; belonging to M.ʳ Tho.ˢ Smith
of Woodhall
Taken in. April 1792. when 7 Years old.

129

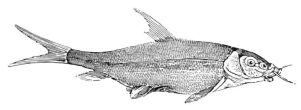

The Barbel

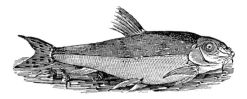

The Gudgeon

Audubon Meets Bewick

About the middle of April I reached Newcastle-upon-Tyne, on my way to London. The Lark was in full song. The Blackbird rioted in the exuberance of joy. The farmer was cheerfully pursuing his labours. Although a stranger in a foreign land, I was delighted with all around me. I had made kind, courteous friendships, and entertained hopes that these would continue. I was not disappointed. I had looked forward to meeting the celebrated engraver on wood, Thomas Bewick, whose works mark the start of an era in the history of art.

Bewick must have heard of my arrival at Newcastle before I had time to call. For he sent his son to me with the following note: 'T. Bewick's compliments to Mr Audubon, and he will be glad of the honour of his company this day to tea at 6 o'clock.' His few words at once revealed his kindly nature.

I had seen little of the town and until I set out with Bewick's son had never crossed the Tyne. First the fine church of St Nicholas caught my eye. Beyond an arched stone bridge lay the wharves and ships, some American vessels among them. The shores were pleasant, the ground undulating. I noticed windmills and glassworks among the buildings. On the Tyne were odd boats manned by long oars and heavily laden with local produce.

At once I was shown to the old engraver in his workshop. Tall, stout, full of life although seventy-four, he came forward to welcome me with a hearty handshake like the perfect Englishman he was. For a moment he removed his cotton nightcap that the coals of Newcastle had soiled a little, and bared his large head. His smiling eyes were set farther apart than any I had ever seen. He had been at work on a small vignette on a block of boxwood, about two by three inches. It represented a dog frightened by spectres, in the night, among rocks, and the roots and branches of trees, and other things that resembled men [see p.131]. Like all his works this curious piece was exquisite. I felt strongly tempted to ask for a whittled fragment.

133

Upstairs all the best artists of Newcastle had assembled. But first I was introduced to the amiable and affable Bewick ladies. A miniaturist who had finished a well-drawn portrait of the engraver was among those present. The old gentleman and I remained beside each other, he to talk of my drawings, I of his woodcuts. Now and then he would take off his cap and draw up his gray-worsted stockings to his knee breeches. But when our conversation became animated the cap stuck to the back of his head as if by magic. The neglected hose resumed their downward trend. His fine eyes sparkled. The free, vivacious way that he voiced his sentiments pleased me enormously. Having heard that my drawings had been exhibited in Liverpool he expressed anxiety to see some. This wish I proposed to gratify next morning.

I asked Bewick where I could obtain a copy of his *Quadrupeds* for my sons in Kentucky, a work which they wished to own. Immediately he answered – 'Here!' – and presented me with a beautiful set.

The tea-drinking came to an end. Young Bewick brought out his new Durham bagpipes and, to amuse me, played some Scottish, English and Irish airs, all sweet and pleasing to my taste. I could scarcely understand how his large fingers managed to cover each separate hole. The sound put me in mind of a hautboy. It had none of the shrill, warlike booming of the pipes of the military Scotch Highlanders heard in Edinburgh.

That night when I parted from Bewick I knew I parted from a friend.

I received another note from him while I was showing some callers my drawings in town. It was an invitation which I understood to mean dinner. Judge of my surprise on discovering at 5 o'clock that, despite my arrival with an appetite becoming the occasion, tea was served. However, the mistake was speedily cleared up to the satisfaction of all concerned. An abundant supply of eatables was placed on the table. A local clergyman joined us. At first the conversation wandered in desultory fashion. But after the repast Bewick took his place by the fire and the two of us discussed our more immediate

134

concerns. I was invited to return for breakfast at 8 a.m., by which time I found the whole family so kind and attentive that I felt quite at home.

Bewick laughed that he would show me how easy it was to cut wood. I soon saw, however, that cutting in his style and method was no joke, easy though he wished it to seem. He himself had made all his delicate and beautiful tools. I may say, with truth, that his shop was the only artist's 'shop' I ever found perfectly clean and tidy. He subscribed for my work in behalf of the local Literary and Philosophical Society; but in this his own enthusiasm misled him, for the learned body did not see fit to ratify the act.

Soon again he invited me back to Gatehead. 'I could not bear the idea of your going off without telling you, in writing, what I think of your *Birds of America*,' he said. 'Here it is in black and white, and make what use of it you may, if any.' I put the unsealed letter in my pocket, and prize it as much as a manuscript, the *Synopsis of the Birds of America*, that Wilson gave me when he was in Kentucky. We chatted a while about natural history. Now and then he would start up exclaiming, 'Oh to be young again – I would go to America too. Hey! what a country it will be, Mr Audubon.'

'Hey what a country it is already, Mr Bewick!' I retorted.

He drank my health and the peace of the world in hot brandy toddy. I returned the compliment by wishing the health of all our enemies. His daughters enjoyed the scene. They had not seen their father in better spirits in years, they said.

On my next and last visit, when we parted, Bewick repeated three times, 'God preserve you, God bless you!' He must have seen how moved I was, even though I could not reply.

A few weeks before his death about a year and a half later, the engraver and his daughters paid me a call in London. I was far from thinking that this interview would be our last and that the death of Bewick, who looked so well, would soon be announced in the papers.

My opinion of this remarkable man is that he was a son of Nature, purely and simply, and that to it he owed nearly all that characterized him as man and artist. Warm in his affections, of deep feeling, highly imaginative, keenly observing, he needed little else to make him what he became: the first English engraver on wood. Where is anything livelier to be found than the vignettes of Bewick, now of the glutton that precedes the Great Black-backed Gull, now the youngsters flying their kite, or the disappointed sportsman who by shooting a Magpie has lost his chance at a woodcock, or the horse trying to reach water, the bull roaring near the fence-style; the poor beggar attacked by the rich man's mastiff? Every leaf of his admirable books excites admiration. Perhaps no one has equalled him in his peculiar path. Thomas Bewick may be rivalled or even excelled in after years, but he must forever be considered, in the art of engraving on wood, what Linnaeus is to natural history. While not the founder he was yet the benefactor, enlightened exponent, and illustrious advocate.

John James Audubon
Ornithological Biography (1831)

Notes

Engravings are identified as a, at the top of the page, b, etc. References to Bain are to his two-volume edition of *The Watercolours and Drawings...*

27a Samples from *The only method to make Reading Easy, or Child's Best Instructor; Containing Emblematic Cuts for the Alphabet......* by T. Hastie, Schoolmaster.

27b 'The Hound and the Huntsman', one of Bewick's prizewinning cuts. *Fables by the late Mr Gay...* was printed by Thomas Saint in Newcastle, 1779.

38b Either very early work by Bewick, or by an apprentice.

40b Note the gibbet in the background, a sign of Bewick's disapproval of the itinerant showman's cruelty to his animals.

46a The initial at the bottom left is Bewick's own; the four on the right refer to the men strolling over the bridge: William Preston, printer; Vint of Whittingham, whose name appears on the dog's collar; John Bell and Bewick himself.

55a This shows the Newcastle arms on a boundary stone, with keels (coal boats) on the River Tyne. Robert Robinson in *Thomas Bewick, His Life and Times* (1887) remarks that the blackbird is 'apropos of coaly Tyne'.

55b The drawing in Bain (2, 140) shows how much Bewick added when he came to engrave the subject: the flight of fieldfares overhead; the heron, crow and magpie nailed to the barn-end as 'scarers'; and the number of bird and animals included increases to over forty.

56c Robinson identifies the boy on the stool as Bewick himself, whose 'little window at my bedhead' may be seen at the end of the house.

57c There is a sequel to this engraving of the runaway cart, showing the cart at a gibbet, in the devil's presence. The idle carter will thus get his just deserts for leaving his cart unattended while drinking at the inn.

59a   The man drinking from the brim of his hat is identified by Jane Bewick as her father. The inscription reads 'Thanks be to the Highest', with a heart cut below.

60b   The engraving is by Luke Clennell from a pencil study by Bewick. The inscription reads 'Too late, but in earnest' (or as T.S.R. Boase suggests, 'Too late to mend'). Jane Bewick annotated this: 'I've heard my Father say an officer hung himself in Benwell dean; the dog is apprehensive' (Bain, 2, 149).

64a   Jane Bewick calls this 'Joe Liddell tracing a hare', Liddell being a boyhood friend of Bewick, who is himself sketched in behind the hedge (Bain, 1, 161).

64b   A dead horse is visible in the background, appropriately, as magpies feed on carrion.

67b   The engraving is by Luke Clennell (1781-1840), who was apprenticed to Bewick from 1797 to 1804, and contributed many tail-pieces to the second volume of *British Birds*.

68b   The engraving is by Charlton Nesbit (1775-1838), who contributed to *British Birds* and *Poems by Goldsmith and Parnell* before he left for London in 1799.

69a   The Redwing is a bird for the pot, and in the background Bewick shows a hunter on his way to bag it.

71a   Jane Bewick annotated this: 'Three Idle lads and a wicked ignorant old fellow, a Tanner have tied a tin kettle to the tail of a poor dog it is in the utmost terror – This in a cathedral City. – This Cut was a long time unfinished. In our early morning walks we often passed a Tannery at the Westgate . . . and my Father watched to see how the leather was placed on the Mans ancles – before he would finish the Cut.'

73c   The woman hanging up her clean washing has refused to give anything to the beggars: they retaliate by opening the gate, and in rush piglets and hens, whose prints can already be seen on a clean shirt. Engraved by Clennell.

76a   This engraving by Luke Clennell is among those referred to by Jane Eyre.

77b   The date on the stone, 4 June 1795, is the birthday of George III, and Jane Bewick notes that the man is 'helplessly drunk' in honour of the occasion (Bain, 2, 146). Robinson identifies him as Rennoldson, a miller from Jesmond. The two crows above suggest that the drunk is only fit for carrion.

79b   Bain interprets this thumbprint as forbidding us to see what happens when the horseman – just visible on the left – reaches the cottage, cf. the leaf in another engraving (not reproduced in this selection), which obscures the 'howdie' (midwife) galloping to a childbirth. Zerner and Rosen offer a more symbolic reading.

82b   The tombstone is inscribed 'Vanity of vanities, all is vanity'. Jane Bewick, in her note on the ruined chapel on the left-hand side, says that it was set on fire 'by the mob – when Butcher Willy [Cumberland] led his Troops thro' Newcastle to Culloden' (Bain, 2, 147).

86b   The wall in this engraving is typical of the fragments of Roman wall found in Bewick's area of Northumbria.

89a   Jane Bewick noted beside this: 'The Hen has brought out four Ducklings. The old proverb says, "If you put another man's child in your bosom, it will creep out at your Sleeve"! – My Mother's Mother taught her this – She, my Grandmother Elliot took an Infant whose Mother had died, and nursed it with her own baby. When the Father came to take it away he *abused her roundly*' (Bain, 2, 151).

89b   Of this engraving of two cockerels sparring, Jane Bewick remarks, 'The Game Cock has the best of it. The hens are never troubling themselves about the fight' (Bain, 2, 155).

91b   Jane Bewick is slightly sententious: 'The old Soldier is very hungry, his friend the dog still more so. – He has lost a leg in fighting the Battles of his Country. I would not say "in the *service* of his Country" for that is very problematical...' (Bain, 2, 154). Note that the peacock sitting on the wall of the rich man's house is better fed than the soldier.

92a   Julia Boyd in her *Bewick Gleanings* quotes from Thomas

Hugo's account of the drawing of the pintado: '...he made the sketch while out walking, between five and six o'clock on a fine summer morning. The gate of the yard being fastened, he had to climb over the wall to obtain an entrance, and has represented this incident in the background to the cut. Though very minute, the resemblance to himself of the figure on the wall is quite perfect.'

93a Jane Bewick points out that 'The old man cannot see, and the boy leading him cannot read; the little dog knows the way instinctively' (Bain, 2, 156).

95b Note the 'geldard' in the foreground: a circular snare, made like a sieve, with horsehair or thin wire. A long string was attached to a stick which supported it above scattered bait. You can see under the trees some boys waiting for the success of their lure.

96c A proof of this engraving of a yoked sow whose piglets are rushing into a garden has a sentence in Bewick's hand: 'How can ye expect the bairns will be honest when the mother's a thief?' (Bain, 1, 166). The first piglet is transfixed by his own reflection in the glass cloche.

99c This is what Bewick called a 'pen & ink facsim', i.e. it reproduces a pen drawing on the wood block, line for line.

101b Engraving by Luke Clennell. Note his treatment of rock surfaces, as compared to Bewick's, also of foliage. You will see that the outer edges of the leaves come within a quite clearly defined arc, whereas Bewick – as in the background to the Night Heron, above – is freer in his handling.

104a Also by Clennell. The fisherman has a 'leister' for salmon spearing, and is using it to pole himself along, with a float for each foot.

104b The angler has 'set gads', that is, fixed-stake fishing lines along the bank.

105b Engraving by Clennell. See how his foliage lines tend in one direction, as also in 106c.

109a   This tailpiece to the kingfisher, a man carrying a coffin inscribed 'A wonderful fish', is singled out in Llewelyn Powys's essay on Bewick as 'evidently intended to remind us of another kind of fishing which daily takes place under the sun' (*Thomas Bewick 1753-1828*, published by the Gravesend Press, Lexington KY, 1951).

110c   Clennell's work.

114b   Apprentice work.

115a   This was originally an *ex libris* for Parson Cotes, vicar of Bedlington, which Bewick has economically re-used by blanking out the rock face.

118b & 123a   Both engravings by Clennell.

119c   Iain Bain has suggested to me that this may be by Isaac Nicholson (1789-1841), apprenticed to Bewick 1804-11, after which he continued to work in Newcastle.

125b   The frogs are engraved by an apprentice, but Ruskin uses them as an example of Bewick's own skill; he 'has set himself to show in all, but especially in the speaker, essential frogginess of mind – the marsh temper.'

125c   This would also have been engraved by an apprentice, however Bewick explained its genesis to Dovaston (20 September 1826): 'while I was a School Boy – it was a custom among rude wild Girls frequently thus to play or amuse themselves, in high Winds, by pressing against it and filling their Gown Skirts like sails – on this occasion these two idle ones, neglecting their knitting & the child – while thus amusing themselves, they repeated a rhyme about "dizzy dizzy dandy"..."sugar candy"..."my *Mimsey* & my Grandy" &c but I have forgot particulars – but the main jet of it amounted to this, that they would enjoy themselves as well as they could, while their mother and their Grandy had trotted off to Church on some business, as useless and foolish as that they were engaged in.'

126a   This was the tailpiece for the fable of the envious and the covetous man; the latter's 'insatiable cravings are at once unaccountable, miserable and absurd' – thus the dog who wants the moon.

127   So that copies would not go missing from the printer or the warehouse, Bewick issued a receipt with every copy of the *Fables of Aesop*. He controlled the copperplate printing of the seaweed overprint, which he engraved and kept. If copies of the letter-press-printed scene (of the Windmill Hills, Gateshead) got out without the rust-coloured overprint, they had been stolen by the printer or his men.

131b   The block that Aubudon saw Bewick engraving on his visit in 1827 (see Appendix).

132   Jane Bewick identified this engraving of 'The Ferry waiting for the Coffin' as her father's last. It is reminiscent of the Eltringham ferry ready to cross the Tyne to Ovingham churchyard (Bain, 1, 198).